Why Do We Have Seasons?

 WHY IS IT **Winter?**

Sara L. Latta

Enslow Elementary

an imprint of

 Enslow Publishers, Inc.

40 Industrial Road
Box 398
Berkeley Heights, NJ 07922
USA

http://www.enslow.com

Words to Know

ice crystal (KRIH stuhl)—Water vapor that turns into ice.

hibernation (hy bur NAY shun)—A time of deep sleep.

season (SEE zuhn)—One of the four parts of the year. Each season has a certain kind of weather.

tilt—To tip to one side. Earth tilts as it goes around the sun.

Earth is tilted.

contents

What is Winter?

Brrr—bundle up! It is winter, the coldest time of the year. Winter is one of the four seasons. The other seasons are spring, summer, and fall.

fall

summer

spring

winter

When is it Winter in North America?

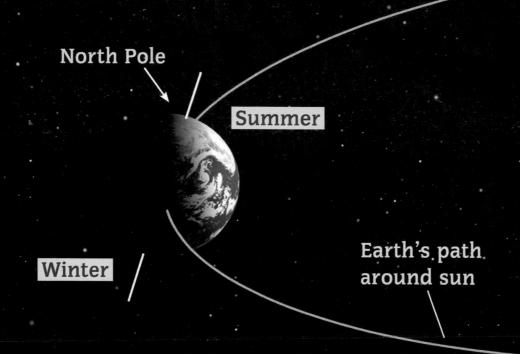

North Pole

Summer

Winter

Earth's path around sun

The earth goes around the sun one time each year. Earth tilts as it goes around the sun.

Winter in North America lasts from around December 21 to March 21.

North Pole

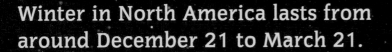

Winter

Summer

When it is winter in the north part of Earth, it is summer in the south part of Earth!

When the North Pole tilts away from the sun, it is winter in North America.

Why is winter weather cold?

The north part of Earth tilts away from the sun in winter. So, the sun's rays hit this part of Earth at an angle.

Rays on an angle are not as strong as rays that fall straight on Earth. So, winter sunlight is not as strong as summer sunlight.

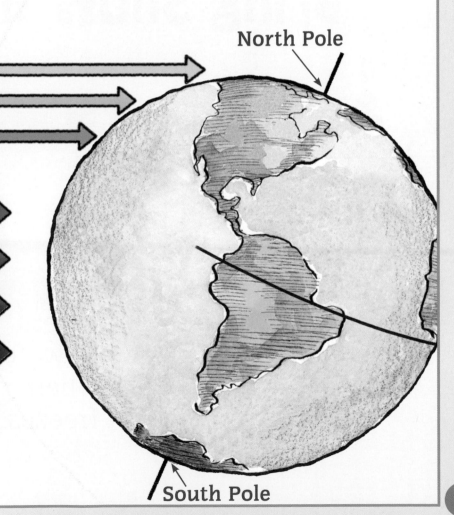

Here, the sun's rays hit Earth on an angle. These rays are not as strong. It is winter in the north part of Earth.

Here, the sun's rays hit Earth directly. Direct light is stronger than light at an angle. It is summer.

North Pole

South Pole

Why Does Winter Weather Bring Snow and Ice?

Earth gets fewer hours of sunlight in the winter. Less sunlight makes the air, water, and land get colder. When water is very cold, it freezes.

In the winter, water in the clouds can freeze into tiny ice crystals. The ice crystals form snowflakes. Water on lakes and ponds may also freeze in the winter.

This is a photo of real snow crystals.

What happens to Plants in the Winter?

In the coldest parts of North America, trees and other plants may stop growing during the winter. They are resting. Their leaves may fall off. Plants live off the food they store in their roots.

Some trees stay green all year. They are called evergreens.

evergreen trees

13

Where Do animals go in the winter?

There are not many growing plants for animals to eat in the winter. Some animals go to warmer parts of the earth where there is plenty of food.

Millions of monarch butterflies fly to Mexico for the winter.

Birds, squirrels, and other animals may search for seeds left on plants.

Bohemian waxwing bird

What is hibernation?

Bears and other animals spend much of the cold winter months curled up in dens. They enter a deep sleep called hibernation.

These two brown long-eared bats are hibernating.

They live off the fat they have stored in their bodies. When they come out of their dens in the spring, they are hungry!

A grizzly bear sits outside its den.

What Do People Do in the Winter?

Winter snow brings winter fun. If you live in a part of the country where it gets cold, you may go sledding or ice skating. You may build a snowman. Sometimes school is closed!

A salty solution to icy streets?

You will need:

- ❄ 2 ice cubes
- ❄ 2 bowls or cups
- ❄ salt
- ❄ clock or watch

1. Put one ice cube in each bowl.

2. Pour some salt over one ice cube. Add nothing to the second ice cube.

3. Check the ice cubes every ten minutes. Which ice cube melts the fastest? Can you guess why people put salt on the streets and sidewalks in the winter?

Learn More

Books

Fleming, Denise. *The First Day of Winter*. New York: Henry Holt and Company, LLC, 2005.

McKneally, Ranida T. and Lin, Grace. *Our Seasons*. Massachusetts: Perfection Learning, 2007.

Smith, Siân. *Changing Seasons*. Illinois: Heinemann-Raintree, 2009.

Learn More

Web Sites

"Enchanted Learning"
<http://www.enchantedlearning.com/crafts/winter/>
Creative and enchanting children's crafts for all seasons.

"Primary Games"
<http://www.primarygames.com/seasons/seasons.htm>
This web site offers a fun and interactive way to learn the four seasons.

"Holidays.Kaboose"
<http://holidays.kaboose.com/winter/>
This web site is filled with winter crafts and recipes for children.

Index

A
animals, 14, 15, 16

B
birds, 15

C
clouds, 11

E
Earth, 6
Earth's tilt, 6, 8
evergreens, 12

H
hibernation, 16

I
ice, 10
ice crystals, 11

L
lakes and ponds, 11
leaves, 12

M
Mexico, 14
monarch butterflies, 14

N
North America,
  6–7, 12
North Pole, 7

P
plants, 12, 14, 15

S
seasons, 4
seeds, 15
snow, 10
snowflakes, 11
sun, 6–7
sunlight, 8, 9, 10

W
water, 10, 11
weather, 8, 10

Enslow Elementary, an imprint of Enslow Publishers, Inc.

Enslow Elementary® is a registered trademark of Enslow Publishers, Inc.

Copyright © 2012 by Sara L. Latta

All rights reserved.

No part of this book may be reproduced by any means without the written permission of the publisher.

Original edition published as *What Happens in Winter* in 1996.

Library of Congress Cataloging-in-Publication Data

Latta, Sara L.
  Why is it winter? / Sara L. Latta.
    p. cm. — (Why do we have seasons?)
    Includes index.
    Summary: "Read about when is it winter in North America, Why winter weather is cold, Where do animals go in the winter and what do people do in the winter"—Provided by publisher.
    ISBN 978-0-7660-3988-9
    1. Winter—Juvenile literature. I. Title.
    QB637.8.L39 2011
    508.2097—dc23   2011019334

Paperback ISBN 978-1-59845-391-1
ePUB ISBN 978-1-4645-0484-6
PDF ISBN 978-1-4646-04884-3

Printed in the United States of America.

092011 Lake Book Manufacturing, Inc., Melrose Park, IL

10 9 8 7 6 5 4 3 2 1

To Our Readers: We have done our best to make sure all Internet addresses in this book were active and appropriate when we went to press. However, the author and the publisher have no control over and assume no liability for the material available on those Internet sites or on other Web sites they may link to. Any comments or suggestions can be sent by e-mail to comments@enslow.com or to the address on the back cover.

♲ Enslow Publishers, Inc., is committed to printing our books on recycled paper. The paper in every book contains 10% to 30% post-consumer waste (PCW). The cover board on the outside of each book contains 100% PCW. Our goal is to do our part to help young people and the environment too!

Note to Parents and Teachers: The **Why Do We Have Seasons?** series supports the National Science Education Standards for K–4 science. The Words to Know section introduces subject-specific vocabulary words, including pronunciation and definitions. Early readers may need help with these new words.

Photo Credits: AP Images/ Fa Zhi, p. 19; Mark Garlick/Science Photo Library, pp. 6–7; © 2011 Photos.com, a division of Getty Images. All rights reserved. pp. 8, 10, 12-15, 17–18, 20–23; Shutterstock.com, pp. 4 (snow crystals), 11, 16 Tom Labaff, p. 9.

Cover Photo: ©2011 Photos.Com, a division of Getty Images. All rights reserved.

Science Consultant, Harold Brooks, PhD, NOAA/National Severe Storms Laboratory, Norman, Oklahoma

Series Literacy Consultant, Allan A. De Fina, PhD, Past President of the New Jersey Reading Association, Professor, Department of Literacy Education, New Jersey City University